Shrieking Flowers

Alivia Nytko

Presentation by *BookLeaf Publishing*

Web: www.bookleafpub.com

E-mail: info@bookleafpub.com

ISBN: 9789357440363

First edition 2023

ACKNOWLEDGEMENT

Thank you to my family, friends, and advisors who have always supported my strong, crazy spirit and my even crazier ideas.

Female Rage

Staring in the mirror
Only cold calculated rage stares back
Finally boiling to the surface
Ready to attack

The siege comes as a single tear running down
her cheek
She wipes it away
How feeble
How meek

What would they say if they saw her cry more
Too emotional for power
"She could start a war"

She thinks to herself that men have started wars
for less
But still her emotions quell at her bequest

And so once again she becomes a traitor to
herself
Grace replaced
Waiting for the right time to strike
A killer with a painted face

Wise Beauty

Skin crinkling a million times before
Forming deep lines of joy and expression
A face that has lived
And continues to tell the tale
What a beauty is aging
A sign of life lived well

Eternal Youth

3

Clang, clink, tinkle, rattle
The sounds of wealth worms their way into my
ear

Flash, glint, shimmer, sparkle
I'm blinded by the counterfeit opulence glued to
the painted husks of the affluent

Chatter, giggle, murmur, squeal
They sell and scheme to promise eternal youth
To point out your doubts and worries that may
be fixed with a simple purchase to stay alive
They'll continue to remind you that 40 is the new
25

Rust

I envy the perpetual softness of the river
The way in which it ebbs and flows with
challenge and grace
Yet it holds itself steady
Still a slave to an unknown race

I envy the power of a mighty storm
The wild carelessness of passionate and
dangerous wind
Yet it brings only damage
Leaving the heart forever dimmed

Yet, I envy the cryptic rust above all
The silence of its calculated invasion
Omnipresent yet unseen
Until it works its way into the center
Slowly cleaving everything between

Simple as Breathing

5

An unconscious love
Comprised of beautifully intertwining souls
Seeing that same beauty
Mirrored in the way that eyes squint and dimples
arise with laughter
And in the way that only the heart can feel
Without giving the mind the knowledge of
interpretation

Vain Ignorance

6

The flowers sprout and scream
Their shrieks seem like a dream
I pick one up
I've had enough
I'll turn it into a moisturizing cream

An Excuse for the Burn

7

Scalding water hitting the skin
Revealing raw flesh from within
The perfect mixture of pleasure and pain
Relishing in the fiery rain

Sloughing off the dirt and sludge
The true grime beneath the heat does not budge

Daughter of the Sun and Moon

Daughter of the sun and moon
Too spirited for complacency
And too peaceful for war
She will be forgotten in favor of a promise of
more

Forever trapped in the cosmos
She will watch and cry
As the sons of mars sever peace and bleed the
land dry

They shout their atrocities as gifts to building a
better world
But they do not listen to the wind or feel the soil
beneath their feet
They only pillage and kill
Lusting for their next easy treat

And so is the daughter of the sun and moon
forced to witness the rise of this false fame
She screams from her tiny corner of the universe
at the savage acts done in her name

Anxiety

I sweat and shiver
My insides like rot
I ask you if it feels hot
You say it is not

I hear whispers and feel eyes
I begin to sway
I ask to leave but you tell me to stay

I ache for a response to all of these words
But nothing comes forward
Only silence is heard

And you are always surprised
Try though I may
"Why must you always be this way?!"

Hive Mind

Collective consciousness experiencing the
universe
At all times
In all places
When you criticize me
You criticize you

Intermission

11

Oh the joy of the sun on my skin
I bake and burn until I make my head spin
Sitting still like a lizard
Or a very tan wizard
Maybe I've had too much gin

Second Puberty

Eyes pucker
Smearing the pigment
Legs bleed
As the razor glides over
Always striving to be older

Now the natural color that stains the eyes
And the hair that crawls up the legs takes on
new meaning

A woman learning to be a child
No longer a slave to her own vicious preening

Bimbofication

13

Rebelling against oppression
With haughty aggression
Exhaustion comes quick
It's hard being a feminist chick
I think I'll be a bimbo for my next profession

Pearl

Let me tell you of a story long ago
When a stray parasite worked its way inside
It burrowed deep into my soul
Looking for a place to hide

Although I felt broken and only have whole
I worked for long years to make sure beauty
would still grow

And after that struggle of transforming pain into
love
A hand reached down and plucked me from
above
It ripped me apart to retrieve the piece of me I
most covet
And to the bottom of the sea I was left to
plummet

Now what is left of me is used to adorn the
necks of others
While my plight is forgotten in favor of show
So how did you get here?
Is it a similar story of suffering and woe?

"Let me tell you a story"

Says the other pearls next to me
Stringed tightly and lined in a row

15

Heart Sick

16

Seizing the body
Infecting the brain
Spreading through the blood
Such is the poison of love

Rarity

The rare flower valued for its beauty
Protected so that all may bear witness
Forgetting its unique contributions beneath the
surface

And in such what a hapless fate is being rare
To be valued for your flora without a true care
Of how you survive
How you live as you choose
In a system that does not see your function
A system in which you lose

Generational Wounds

18

She smiles as she looks upon her greatest love
The new life she has given a precious soul from
above

She prays that this relationship would heal her
own childhood wound
By raising a child
She could transform her anger into something
that would flourish into beauty soon

But the child becomes a reflection of
remembrance
One she cannot control
And so she takes up the spot of her own mother
Fulfilling her destined role

Silly Little Tragedy

Little boxes
Decorated with the brightest hues
In these boxes you can be whatever you may
choose

A doctor
Traveler
Veterinarian
Or monk
You can even run around pretending you're a
skunk!

And after many years
Filled with tears
Cheers
And Fears
The door to escape the box will soon disappear

You'll begin to wonder why
To look up at the painted sky
Carefully crafted by unseen puppeteers

Infinite Questions

Beginning and ending with questions
A question to live
A question to die
A question to know
And a question to wonder why

Diverging roads these questions lead
Some will break you down
Some will leave you freed

But to not answer any is a terrible shame
Pursuit of an answer is a light to a flame
To illuminate and guide
In unknowing stillness you will reside

Until one day a spark
An answer not yet complete
For another question has formed
Leading down a new street